# Jai's Crown

Written By
Dr. Kyerra Oglesby

Illustrated By
Gaurav Bhatnagar

# This book belongs to

_____

# Jai's Crown

Written by Dr. Kyerra Oglesby
Copyright © 2023 by
Dr. Kyerra Oglesby

ALL RIGHTS RESERVED. NO part of this book may be reproduced or transmitted in any form by any means, electronic or mechanical, including photocopying and recording, or by any information storage and retrieval system, except as may be expressly permitted in writing from the author.

Paperback ISBN: 978-1-7364036-2-4
eBook ISBN : 978-1-7364036-3-1

Printed in the United States of America

Illustrated and designed by Gaurav Bhatnagar
www.ePublishingexperts.com

## - Dedication -

I dedicate this book to my daughter, who is not afraid to be herself.  She boldly defines and refines who she is using her own rules. Jai, may you continue to shine bright under the pride of your crown.

All during math, Molly pulled at my hair. I knew it was her, but every time I turned around she acted as if she were busy working. I raised my hand to tell Mrs. Brown, but she never looked in my direction. Every time I got on the bus, my friends would tell me all about how they saw Molly pulling my hair in class.

Each day, I would tell mommy all about Molly pulling my hair. Mommy always knew how to explain things to me so that I felt better about bad situations. "Perhaps she is just curious", said Mommy as she softly brushed my hair in place. "People always ask me if my hair is real. They want to know what it feels like. Sometimes they even ask me if they can touch it."

One day I was telling Mommy about Molly. "Isn't all hair the same?" I asked. "In some ways it is. All hair lives. It should be kept clean and healthy. But, the hair on our head is like a crown. Almost like wearing a magical crown." said Mommy. "Magical Crown?", I asked in disbelief. "Magical crown," emphasized Mommy. "Hair is diverse and versatile. It can be changed, you can cut it to make it shorter or add to it to make it longer. Your hair sits on top of your head much like a crown. When you disrespect your hair by being ashamed or embarrassed because your hair does not look like someone else's hair, you are tilting your crown. A tilted crown does not exude any magic. It is okay to admire or be curious about someone else's hair. You can't control others, but you have a magical crown that you can wear upright on your head without being ashamed. Being uncomfortable and ashamed of your hair tilts your crown. Hair confidence keeps your crown upright. Never allow anyone's taunting to make you tilt your crown. Come with me," said Mommy.

Mommy took me into the bathroom where she began to wash her waist-length hair. Magically mommy's hair went from straight to curly. It began to coil as soon as she placed her head underneath the running water. She let me pour the shampoo right onto her head. Mommy shrieked and giggled as the cold shampoo landed on her scalp.

As Mommy brushed and dried her hair, magically, it stretched and coiled back and forth like waves in the ocean. Next, Mommy parted her hair and made four large plaits. One by one, she unraveled the plaits and

used her blow drier to smooth out the waves until, "poof"! Magically her hair puffed up like giant dirt-covered snow piles.

Soon smoke from the pressing comb filled the air. Mommy pressed my hair every other Sunday morning before church. I knew what came next, I scurried to search under the sink for the pressing oil. I found it just in time to watch Mommy wrap the last of 3 of my barrettes around her hair and reach for me to hand her the pressing oil. I watched in amazement as the giant dirt-covered snow piles turned to shiny, silk ribbons.

As Mommy pressed the last strand of hair, I couldn't help feeling sad thinking about Molly pulling my hair tomorrow.

The next morning, I walked in and sat down right in front of Molly No sooner than I sat in my chair, Molly leaned in and whispered, " If you think those Princess Leia buns are going to keep me out of your hair, you're wrong!" "Look, everyone, Jai is auditioning for a role in Star Wars", Molly announced. Everyone laughed out loud and pointed at me. I slumped down in my seat from embarrassment. All-day Molly constantly pulled at my hair. It hurt so bad because Mommy must have used every bobby pin we had in the house, to keep my hair in place. All-day, the

kids told nothing but Princess Leia jokes. Even my friends were calling me Princess Leia. I started to feel like my crown wasn't magic at all! In fact, it started to feel more like a curse rather than a crown. I couldn't wait to jerk the bobby pins out of my hair and tell Mommy about Molly's continued antics.

Of course, Mommy picked up on my immense sadness as soon as I arrived home with a handful of bobby pins. She said, "You know there is one magic trick we can do with your crown that Molly hasn't seen yet." Mommy winked

at me in a way that let me know I should trust her and not ask any questions. She took my hand and led me into the bathroom toward the sink.

The next day, I didn't wait for the bus. I skipped all the way to school. I wanted to be the first student in my seat, smiling, and ready to show off my magic crown. When I got to school, Mrs. Worthy, the meanest principal on the planet, held the door for me, smiled, and complimented me on how nice I looked.

Brian, the coolest boy in the 5th grade, let me cut in front of him in the breakfast line. Even Mr. Daniels, the most out-of-touch science teacher, told me he liked my hair as we passed one another in the hallway.

When I walked into the classroom, all the students stared. No one said a word, they just looked at me in disbelief. Molly didn't pull my hair in class. No one told a single "Princess Leia" joke the entire day.

Sharon, the coolest girl in the 5th grade invited me to swing on the swingset beside her at recess. Me! Can you believe it? Me! Mommy's magic crown trick was actually working. I was having the best day ever! Until...

The clouds began to hover over the playground like a tent pitched over a campground. Lightning darted across the sky as if it were trying to maintain the lead in a 50-yard dash. Then the worst thing that could ever, ever, EVER happen. Happened.

"RAIN"!!! Screamed Mrs. Toron as she motioned for us to take cover inside the building. I scurried toward the back door of the school, like a squirrel chasing a nut. I ran with all of my might. At least fast enough to avoid being drenched.

As soon as everyone was safe inside, an outburst of laughter roared through the hallway. I was so focused on outrunning the rain, I had missed what seemed to be the funniest joke ever told. But, no, I soon realized that I was the funniest joke. All the students were pointing and laughing. At me! I stood there frozen in the frost of their

laughter. I was in shock. Even Brian and Sharon were laughing and they had been so nice to me earlier. My heart pounded inside my chest like an African drum. I had to get away and fast. I ran to the main office as fast as my legs could carry me.

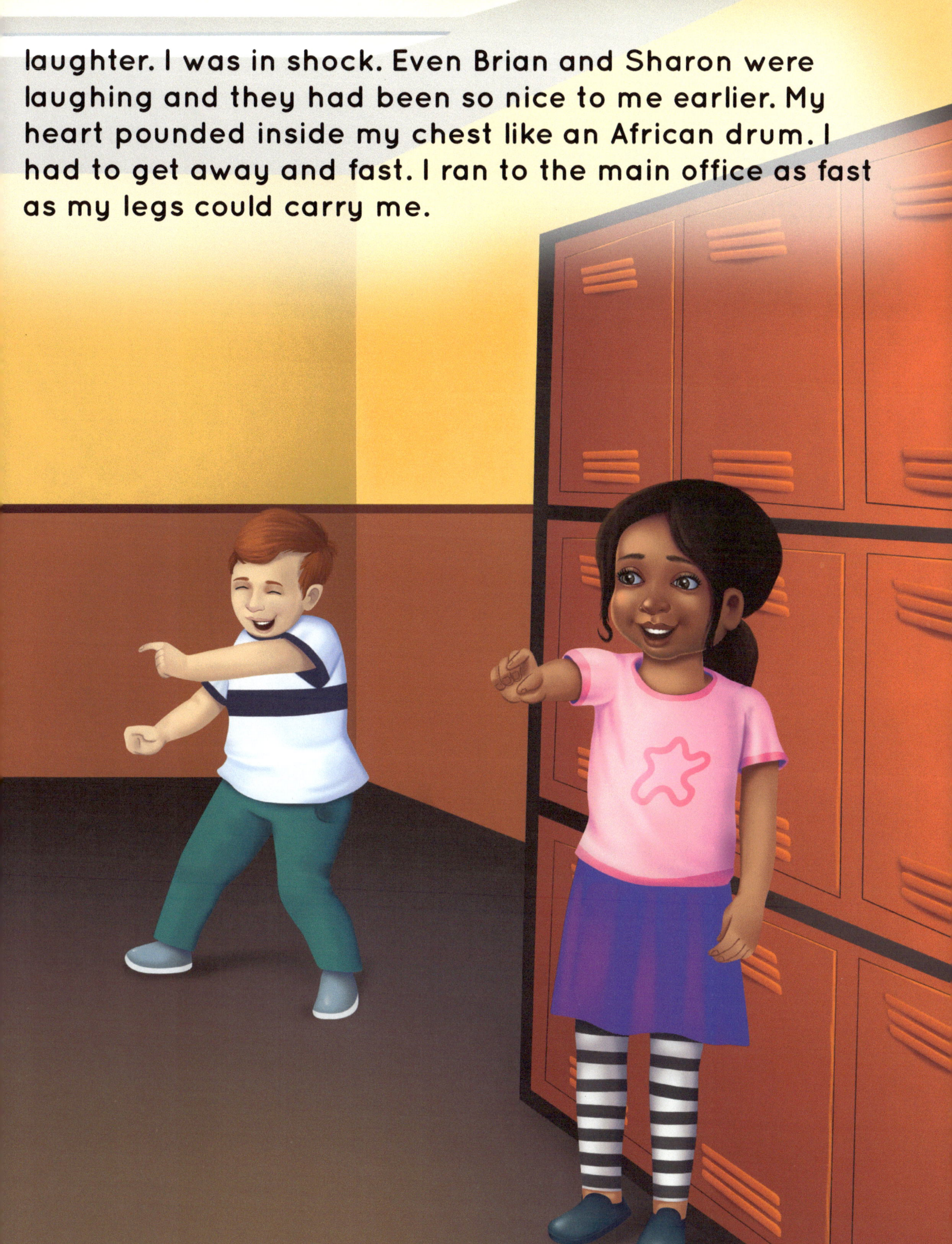

I pounced on the nurse's bed like a cat on a ball of yarn. The tears flowed uncontrollably down my cheeks. I faintly heard Mrs. Brown trying to explain to the nurse what took place. The nurse thought it was best to call my mom.

Mommy appeared shortly after the nurse hung up the phone. I didn't have enough nerve to go back to the classroom and collect my belongings. I just wanted to go home and fast. Mommy tried to encourage me to talk and sing with her on the way home. But, I wasn't in the mood. She helped me change out of my soaked and wet clothes. I showered, slipped on a nightgown, and crawled into bed. I didn't feel like I could take one more minute of this day.

Mommy brought me a large mug of hot chocolate. She even piled it high with marshmallows, which are my favorite. But, I couldn't find the energy to sit up and sip. Mommy pulled out the brush and began stroking my hair. The soft bristles gliding over my scalp did the trick. It was as if the bristles brushed all the stress and sadness I was feeling away and sent me into a deep sleep.

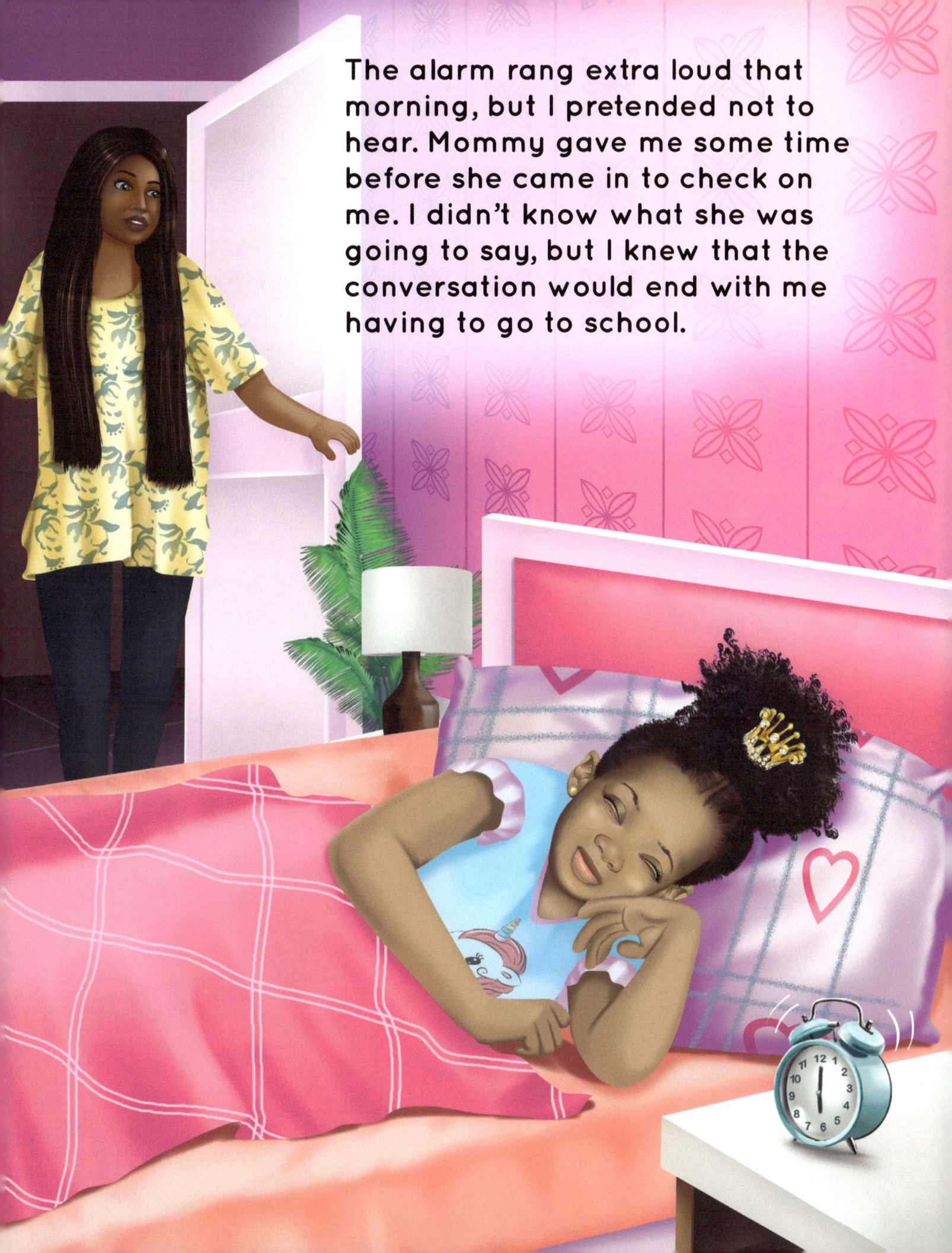

The alarm rang extra loud that morning, but I pretended not to hear. Mommy gave me some time before she came in to check on me. I didn't know what she was going to say, but I knew that the conversation would end with me having to go to school.

I ate my cereal so slowly it was like a bowl of soggy socks by the time I finished eating it. Instead of taking the bus to school, I decided to walk. I didn't want to face my friends after they laughed at me and I especially didn't want to face Sharon, Brian, or Molly.

When I arrived at school, Mrs. Worthy, the meanest principal on the planet, gave me a good talking to about being late. Brian ignored me in the breakfast line. He even took the last cinnamon bun from the serving line and he knew I reached for it first. Mr. Daniels walked right by me in the hall as if I were a ghost.

I tipped in class hoping to sneak into a seat at the back of the room. I sat in an empty seat in the back row, slouched down, with my head ducked into my shoulders. Half an hour had passed and I didn't have a clue what Mrs. Brown was teaching. The next thing I knew, she was calling on me to answer a question. My eyes were focused, but my brain was still swimming in the slush of sadness. I leaned in to get a better look at the board,

but my eyes caught a glimpse of Mrs. Brown. She looked like Mrs. Brown, but she kinda looked like me. At first, I couldn't figure out why I thought she looked like me. But, I soon figured it out. It was her hair, styled like mine. Mrs. Brown was wearing Jai's Crown. In fact, so was Sharon, Bella, Carmela, Terri, Crystal, Kenza, and Nyla. All the girls were wearing Jai's crown. I was overjoyed at how amazing each of them looked. All different in their own way, but amazing just the same.

I realized that each of us is unique and how we wear our hair should not dictate how we are viewed or treated by others. Whether we wear our hair curly, coily, braided, twisted, locced, in an afro, or straightened. Everyone has a crown. We are entitled to wear our

crown as we see fit. My hair is like magic because I can wear it any way I like. I love my crown and won't allow anyone to make me tilt my crown again!

# About the Author

Kyerra had been an educator for over 16 years when she published her first book during the 2020 COVID-19 Pandemic. After being in education for 18 years, she is publishing this book in response to witnessing the effects that bullies, struggles with self-identification, and pressures to conform have on children. Jai's Crown is a story about a young girl with insecurities regarding her natural hair. She grapples with embracing her natural hair while enduring constant teasing at school.

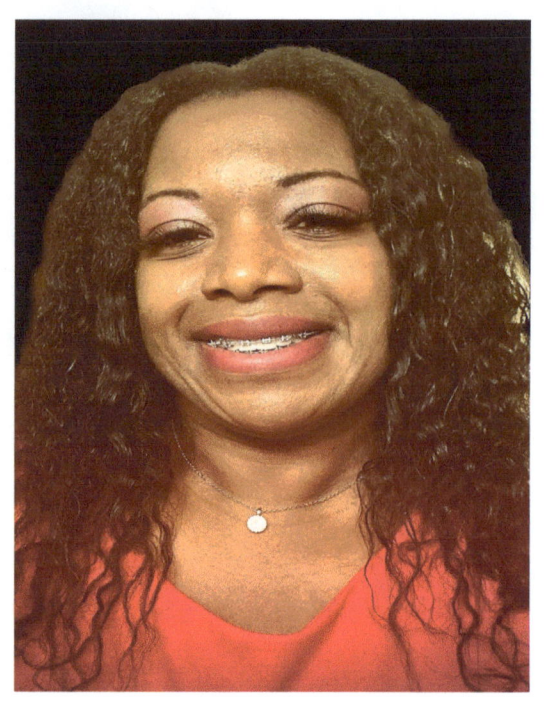

I am an elementary school principal who is passionate about teaching and learning. Also, a mother of 2 children and a boxer pup named Moxie. I began writing stories for children over ten years ago. I finally gained the courage to publish and share my stories with the world. I desire that my stories will motivate, encourage, or inspire anyone who reads them.

www.ingramcontent.com/pod-product-compliance
Lightning Source LLC
Chambersburg PA
CBHW042249100526
44587CB00002B/78